The Oxymoronic God

Anna Townsend

ISBN: 979-8-8316-1377-3

DEDICATION

This book is dedicated to all the readers of my blog, www.dislocatedchristian.org. Your enthusiasm for my thoughts about God has inspired me to produce this book, and I am grateful for each of you.

CONTENTS

THE OXYMORONIC GOD

There are paradoxes and enigmas that exist within God, and these are captured in the oxymorons that describe Him. My hope is that by understanding more about God, we can find encouragement for our lives and the tensions we experience.

A DEFINITION

If it has been a while since you were at school, you may have forgotten what an oxymoron is, but I promise you, it is worth revisiting them. The official definition of an oxymoron is a

"a figure of speech in which apparently contradictory terms appear in conjunction"

That's a relatively dry description, so if it hasn't helped prompt your memory, perhaps some examples will assist. Here are a few:

Open secret. Old news. Only choice. Almost exactly. Deafening silence. Virtual reality. Civil war.

THE BEAUTY OF OXYMORA

As an English as a foreign language teacher, one of my favourite lessons is teaching oxymorons (sorry, oxymora just doesn't sound right) because they can be *seriously funny*. My students love to guess their *obviously hidden* meanings. Every language has its own oxymorons, and my learners are also keen to share the ones they know from their mother tongues.

Most oxymorons consist of two words that mean the opposite of each other; together, they offer a new way of looking at something familiar. In combination, they push aside established definitions so that there is space for curiosity and questions. Just like opposing forces or energies, they combine to create something new.

USING OXYMORONS TO DESCRIBE GOD

Defining God using oxymorons is nothing new. He is the *'Servant King'* and the *'Crucified Saviour'*, both of which have been used to describe Jesus since the first century. When we examine these names closely, I picture each word as a flint. The words strike against each other and create sparks of light that, for an instant, allow us to see God more clearly. The only limitation to doing this is our comprehension and imagination.

There are many more Oxymoronic names of God to wrap our heads around: *Prince of Peace, Living Sacrifice, Unchanging Creator, Divine Human, Jealous God, Lion and Lamb, and Shepherd Lord.*

A SUPER-OXYMORON

The ultimate description of God, though, is the Trinity: Father, Son and Holy Spirit. Strictly speaking, this is not an oxymoron, but it is in the same mould. We could call it a super-oxymoron; three ideas converge to create a thoroughly unique God, like no god that has ever been known before or since.

BLINDING LIGHT

Oftentimes, God's brilliance is too bright for me. Peter Rollins describes it as like looking at the sun. The more I see of God and try to fathom Him, the more overwhelmed I become. It is a beautiful metaphor and explains how I feel about these oxymorons. Sometimes, I just do not get it, and my head hurts!

UN DIEU DÉFINI EST UN DIEU FINI

This is a French saying that means 'A defined God is a finished God'. Oxymorons offer a means of pushing ourselves to understand God more wholly; with faith and the Holy Spirit, our minds grapple with the oxymoronic God and discover new aspects of his character.

TENSIONS AND STUMBLING BLOCKS FOR CHRISTIANS

Oxymorons can cause problems too. Sometimes, these opposing words, or forces, do not create light with which to see God better but behave more like brutes at the end of a rope. They yank us in opposite directions, and we fail to comprehend any overall meaning. So many people leave the church and turn away from God because they cannot draw close to a '*Merciful Judge*' that speaks of '*Foolish Wisdom*'. To them, he is an '*Absent Father*' who has turned his back on a suffering world, and so they become '*Devout Atheists*'.

AN OXYMORONIC GOD HAS OXYMORONIC FOLLOWERS

As Christians, oxymorons have been used to describe us, too and can be just as confusing and challenging. Are we '*sinning saints*' or '*forgiven sinners*'? The answer to this theological question has implications for our identity in Christ and our security as his children.

Additionally, we are called to spread the good news, which could undoubtedly be described as '*Old News*'. How do we maintain the freshness of the gospel? I feel sure that we are not called to be '*Silent Christians*'?

MORE

I delve more deeply into some of the oxymorons I have included above in the following pages. I have written about them in this book, and I hope I have piqued your interest.

WHAT HAVE I MISSED?

If you can think of any other oxymorons used to describe God, Christians or the life of faith, please let me know by visiting my blog www.dislocatedchristians.org.

MEEKNESS AND MAJESTY

Before reading further, you could watch a video of a Graham Kendrick song that I sang as a child. The words are beautiful, and every verse is packed full of oxymoronic ideas and descriptions of God. Just search for 'Meekness and Majesty' on Youtube. Enjoy!

1 PRINCE OF PEACE

We live in a world that tells us we should fight for our rights and that our freedoms need protecting. It's easy to believe that life is one big competition and that many people want to take advantage of us. Yet, that's not how God describes our role in the world; his view is the opposite of this. He calls us to humility, and when things get tough, we are to love our enemies.

Understanding that as Christians, we follow the Prince of Peace helps us find ways to overcome the subtle lies of this world and live in harmony with one another.

The title Prince of Peace was introduced by the prophet Isaiah to describe Jesus and foretell his birth, around 700 years before Jesus was born. So, why is Prince of Peace an oxymoron?

LET'S BEGIN BY EXAMINING THE WORD PRINCE

When Isaiah prophesied, and during the period Jesus was alive, thrones and Kingships were won by might. Only in the last few hundred years have we become used to purely hereditary models of royal lineage.

Princes were expected to fight for their nations and take an active role on the battlefield. There were some exceptions when countries experienced rare periods of peace and stability. Still, the title Prince has been synonymous with Military General, Fighter or Hero for most of history.

Not only were Princes expected to defeat external enemies, but many threats came from within their own families. Kings around the world took multiple wives, and these wives and their sons competed among themselves to inherit their Father's Kingdom. Royal families from every continent and tradition have witnessed vast amounts of bloodshed as princes have vied with each other to win the crown.

In short, being a Prince has not been a very peaceful vocation.

So, when Isaiah pairs the word Prince with Peace, this is new and unusual.

WHAT CAN WE SAY ABOUT PEACE?
There are many verses in the book of Isaiah (where the prophecies of Isaiah are recorded in the Bible) that describe peace.

Creation will rejoice because of the peace that Jesus will establish. Even the mountains will burst into song, and the trees will clap along – Isaiah 55:12. Contrast this to the desolation and death that Princes from the ancient world would leave in their wake after battles and during wars.

Without peace, we are like a restless sea that endlessly churns up dirt and mire – Isaiah 57:20

Peace reaches everywhere; it is all-encompassing; nowhere and no one is left out. It extends from East to West and will overflow from us – Isaiah 45:7 & 66:12

Even the feet of those who bring peace are beautiful – Isaiah 52:7

Peace is granted rather than enforced. Peace enforced through tyranny is no peace at all – Isaiah 26:12

PUTTING PRINCE AND PEACE TOGETHER. WHAT DOES IT MEAN FOR US?
We do not need to strive because the Prince of Peace is a man of action. He will not just keep a lid on our anxieties, and he won't close his eyes to injustice. Instead, He will resolve these situations fully. He will put an end to war and rule righteously; the peace He establishes is certain and long-lasting.

Whom we follow determines the peace we experience (Isaiah 59:8). Let's follow Him.

2 LION AND LAMB

In 2015 I published a book entitled 'Destination Transformation: A forty-day journey to change the world written for people with baggage'. The book aims to help Christians identify their God-given calling and provide some tools for tackling the issues that confront us as we go about meeting the world's needs. Jesus is described as both a Lion and a Lamb, which seems contradictory and oxymoronic, but since we are called to be like Him, how do we decide which we should emulate? On Day 21, the book attempts to answer this question.

DAY 21: ARE YOU A LION OR A LAMB?

By now, I hope that the particular issue or group of people to which you are called to transform is becoming more evident. If you have not reached this point yet, you may want to spend longer going over the last 20 days before moving on.

Once you have identified your calling with a fair degree of clarity, there is a need to define your strategy. Will you take on the world by espousing the characteristics of a lion or those of a lamb? A lion's approach is to get angry, to roar and to fight against injustice. A lamb, on the other hand, sacrifices everything they have for the good of others. Jesus was likened to both a lion and a lamb at different occasions in His ministry. There is nothing to stop us, like Him, bearing both identities. Nonetheless, it is beneficial to think about both approaches and seek God as to which one He might be particularly calling you to take on.

Lions possess two key character traits: they roar, and they are portrayed in the Bible as bold fighters. Whether we choose to enter politics or not, our mission is to 'speak up for those who cannot speak up for themselves', particularly in defence of the destitute and 'for the rights of all the unfortunate' (Proverbs 31:8, NASB). These words were written to King Lemuel by his mother, though biblical scholars cannot be certain who this family were; the words are included here in Proverbs as an example of wise advice given to a king. We, too, are called to royal responsibilities. These are best understood in terms of 1 Peter 2:9: 'But you are a chosen race, a royal priesthood, a holy nation, a people for God's own possession, so that you may proclaim the excellencies of Him who has called you out of darkness into His marvellous light' (NASB). If we heed this advice, then we know that we, too, are called to roar.

Dear Fellow Traveller,

When I realised that I should be roaring, it was liberating. I had grown up in a church where to speak up against injustice was unheard of; it seemed the greatest act one could do for others was to wash up, and I hated washing up! Washing up was held up as the golden standard for anyone wanting to demonstrate they cared about others. I'm not a particularly angry person, but I do have a clear idea of what is right and wrong. As I grew older and discovered that things went on in the world that were just not right, it was hard to see how washing up was going to tackle these bigger issues. Thank God He allows us to roar!

Roarrrr!

Anna

Lions roar to communicate that the territory they are in is occupied. How appropriate for us as well. We, too, can roar to let Satan know that he is straying into ground that belongs to God. Doing this may take the form of lobbying, signing petitions online or taking part in a march. It might mean standing outside a high street shop informing customers of the sweatshop labour used to produce the clothes sold inside. Many Christians steer away from such activities, possibly because they fear these behaviours may be sinful; after all, we are required to honour our leaders in government and authority. Yet we can be assured that 'the righteous are bold as a lion' (Proverbs 28:1, NASB), and ultimately the Lion will triumph (see Revelation 5:5 and Numbers 23).

Coupled with the notion of roaring against injustice is a prophetic role of perceiving and calling forth judgement and salvation. The lion does not just make a lot of noise but calls others to join in the fight and goes on to devour enemies as part of the process of bringing about justice. This is explored in the third chapter of Amos, and we would do well to remember that in many cases of suffering and injustice, there is an equivalent spiritual battle. We are called to fight and should not be afraid. God fights with us, and as CS Lewis famously wrote, 'He's wild, you know. Not like a tame lion'.

Contained within Celtic Daily Prayer, there is a stirring prayer that calls on God to enable us to roar on behalf of others. It is the Prayer of Caedmon, and these powerful lines are repeated several times within it: 'I cannot speak unless you loose my tongue; I only stammer, and I speak uncertainly; but if you touch my mouth, my Lord, then I will sing the story of your wonders!' The prayer elaborates further: 'He [Jesus] said: "How dare you wrap God up in good behaviour, and tell the poor that they should be like you? How can you live at ease with riches and success, while those I love go hungry and are oppressed? It really is for such a time as this that I was given breath." His words were dangerous, not safe or tidy.' Here we see Jesus described as being angry. He is dangerous because He challenges the customary practices of His day. We are called to do likewise, and my hope is that this will be a relief to many of you reading this: we don't need to be tame.

Being a lamb is a powerful and biblical calling too. A lamb represents sacrifice and is completely countercultural to the ways of the world. In transforming the world, you will almost certainly find that you have to relinquish your time, and giving money to causes is one of the best-known sacrificial ways to help others. There is also a sense of sacrifice when we pay more for goods because we choose to buy ethically made or environmentally friendly products. Romans 12:1–2 exhort us to play the role of the lamb in order to understand and bring about God's good will 'Therefore, I urge you, brothers and sisters, in view of God's mercy, to offer your bodies as a living sacrifice, holy and pleasing to God – this is your true and proper worship. Do not conform to the pattern of this world, but be transformed by the renewing of your mind. Then you will be able to test and approve what God's will is – his good, pleasing and perfect will' (NIV).

Jesus is our greatest role model for that of a lamb: He gave His life by dying a brutal death on the cross so that we are saved. He has paid the ultimate sacrifice, but we too have a worthy calling to take part in God's great plan for humankind: 'you also, like living stones, are being built into a spiritual house to be a holy priesthood, offering spiritual sacrifices acceptable to God through Jesus Christ' (1 Peter 2:5, NIV). The biblical mandate is clear – we are to be like Christ, and so sacrifice is to be expected. How much we sacrifice is harder to determine; in giving our time and money to others, we can be tempted to believe that everything rests on us and that the more we give, the more successful we will be at changing lives. Like Abraham, we, too, should remember that 'God himself will provide the lamb for the burnt offering' (Genesis 22:8, NIV).

It is unlikely that the roles of lion and lamb are entirely mutually exclusive, and this is being recognised more and more by Christian organisations. Groups such as Tearfund, Christian Aid, and CAFOD, traditionally seen as merely channels for us to sacrifice money, have passionate advocacy teams that campaign for change and offer individuals many ways to get involved as a lion and a lamb.

ASK YOURSELF

How appropriate is the lion or the lamb role in transforming the situation you are called to? Are there already lions or lambs addressing the situation? How could you help and complement them? Is a change of approach required?

PRAY

Ask God to help you understand the roles of lion and lamb more clearly, and how they apply in the circumstances you wish to see transformed. Pray that God would help you be a lion and/or lamb to achieve His will.

3 MERCIFUL JUDGE

It turns out that the idea of God being a Merciful Judge is extremely difficult to wrap my head around, both theologically and in practice. As a result, it took me ages to think about and write this chapter. Preparing it has also revealed some truths about myself that I don't really like; I've discovered that I'm not all that merciful and prefer others to get their comeuppance.

THE WRONG IDEA

This is how I (wrongly) see things: God can choose how to respond to us, and he swings between judgement on the one hand and mercy on the other. As for me, I find myself not particularly wanting to punish people; however, I do want them to feel the consequences of whatever bad action they have taken.

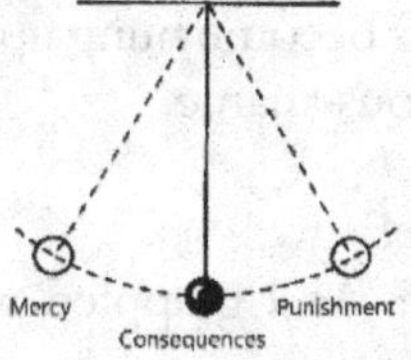

JONAH GOT IT WRONG TOO

I'm not alone in feeling this way; in the Bible, we find the story of Jonah. God asked him to go to a group of foreigners to tell them that how they were acting was wrong. When the Ninevites heeded Jonah's message and repented, God forgave them, and this made Jonah mad. He didn't think the Ninevites deserved to be forgiven and to receive God's mercy.

AN ANGRY OLDER BROTHER

Similarly, in a story that Jesus told, we hear of the anger of an older brother. His younger brother impertinently asks their Father for his share of the inheritance before disappearing for several years. The younger brother squanders everything he has been given on 'sex, drugs and rock'n'roll' before returning home penniless. Yet, their father is delighted to see him and throws a party to welcome him back, infuriating the older brother, who has dutifully remained at home all this time.

BEING HONEST

Now, let's be honest. How many of us are happy when God throws a party for those we deem to be sinners? I know that I am a long way from thinking and acting like God in many situations; in fact, I often think he's too merciful. Why does he permit the war in Yemen to go on and on? What about human trafficking and all forms of abuse? Couldn't he do more to stop them? Sometimes I forget he's a judge at all; I focus on the idea that love wins and don't like the idea of Him being judgmental. However, I've noticed that in other church traditions, the emphasis is on God as Judge and Christians from these backgrounds become hung up on confession and regrettably feel enormous shame.

SO, HOW DOES JESUS DO IT?

How is he both merciful and just? As I grappled with

these questions, it became clear that I needed to understand what God means by Judge and Justice. I have learnt that when God created the world, he intended it to be perfect and for human beings to steward it lovingly. When the fall occurred (sin entered the world), creation became imperfect and out of kilter; the whole fabric of life was disrupted and corrupted. Since then, it has been longing to be how it was supposed to be; the Bible describes the whole world as groaning to be set right. This then is God's idea of justice: the dial is turned from corruption to flourishing. His type of justice is healing, and we can take part in it both individually and collectively. It is impossible to separate God's mercy from his justice. When God's justice meets our brokenness, He responds in mercy.

When Jesus overcame death, it qualified him to become judge of the living and the dead. As a Judge, he doesn't sit in a courtroom wearing a wig and doling out reprimands; instead, he is the prime exemplar of what life looks like when it has been set right. He's our model and precedent. He can mercifully forgive our selfishness and put things right with justice because He has conquered everything that prevents our flourishing. He defeated death, so, rather than having a magic wand to wave away our sins, he offers victory over them and demonstrates an alternative way to live.

IN PRACTICE: JUSTICE, MERCY AND HUMAN TRAFFICKING

What does all this mean in practice? To test my understanding of how justice and mercy can work together, I found that I needed to apply them to a real-life situation. As the chairperson of a charity that helps vulnerable women in Nepal, one of the issues that really riles me is human trafficking. Each year approximately 15,000 young girls (the average age is 13) are trafficked from Nepal to India and are enslaved in brothels. Traffickers deceive the impoverished girls with the promise of domestic work and a chance to provide for their families. Instead, they are raped and imprisoned in the countless brothels that do business in every village, town and city across India. It's not actually the traffickers that enrage me the most; I know they are often poor and frequently oblivious to where the girls will end up and are just pawns in the supply chain. Instead, it is the men that casually frequent the brothels and pay for sex with these young girls that are the objects of my wrath. How dare they! Can't they see how young they are? Don't they realise these girls are somebody's daughters? My instinct is to call on God to strike them all down.

From the definition of merciful justice above, it seems that God would want these men to flourish and to be set right. This would undoubtedly mean that they would have happy and healthy home lives, where they would enjoy peaceful intimacy with their wives. Their minds would be renewed so that they would view all women as precious image-bearers of Christ and therefore respect and esteem them, training their sons and nephews to treat them likewise. As a result, they would work to bring about the flourishing of girls in brothels by working for their release and undoubtedly preventing other men from going to brothels. Men may visit brothels because it is a cultural norm or to improperly meet more profound psychological needs for love and affection. Whatever these needs are and whatever emotional wounds caused them, God would care about them and want to heal them. Ultimately the men would come to know God and his love.

LORD, HAVE MERCY ON ME
As I am re-reading the paragraph I have just written (I am sure I have missed many other ideas), I can see that this response is so much better than swift judgment because it would lead to more right-living and flourishing in the world. I pray for those things I have listed and for these men to

turn from their wicked ways. Lord, have mercy on me because I don't often think like this. Thank you for being a merciful judge.

Many of the ideas in this chapter were based on a sermon given by N.T. Wright. Any theological errors are mine, not his.

4 ABSENT FATHER

I know of no Christian that does not occasionally doubt the goodness of God and whether He is present with them. Some Christians hide these doubts better than others, but they are nothing to be ashamed of. For non-Christians, the feeling that God is an absent Father prevents them from investigating the Christian faith and trusting Him.

Absent Father is included in this exposition of the Oxymoronic names of God because it reveals a grievance against God that Christians do well to understand, both for the strength of their own faith and the faith of others. While the name Absent Father is not a term used directly to describe God in the Bible, it captures an age-old complaint that biblical, historical, and modern-day figures have wrestled with.

As I compose this piece, I am aware that nothing I write will convince you that God is lovingly present. All I can do is encourage you to take your doubts, questions, loneliness, frustrations, and hurts directly to Him. It's even OK to scream, shout, and cry at God. He can take it. You can talk to Him out loud or silently in your head; sometimes, it can help to write Him a letter. However you attempt to communicate with Him, I am confident that He will be delighted that you are seeking Him and would far rather be engaged than ignored.

It turns out that we are in good company when questioning the presence of a Father-like God. What follows is a selection of quotes and questions by well-known persons that I have found helpful when I find myself wondering where God is. I hope you find some echoes of your doubts and questions in them.

ASKING GOD WHEN HE WILL DO SOMETHING

David is a biblical character that came from humble beginnings and eventually became King of Israel. At one point, he was driven out of his home and went on the run. He wrote Psalm 13 when surrounded by his enemies and fearing for his life. Note how he accuses God of being absent and forgetful. David was renowned as a man after God's own heart, so it seems that speaking like this to our heavenly Father is entirely acceptable and even commended by God.

How long, O Eternal One? How long will You forget me? Forever?

How long will You look the other way?

How long must I agonise, grieving Your absence in my heart every day?

How long will You let my enemies win?

Turn back; respond to me, O Eternal, my True God!

Put the spark of life in my eyes, or I'm dead.

My enemies will boast they have beaten me; my foes will celebrate that I have stumbled.

But I trust in Your faithful love; my heart leaps at the thought of imminent deliverance by You.

I will sing to the Eternal, for He is always generous with

me.

Psalm 13

DADDY!

These words were written by the former Archbishop of Canterbury Rowan Williams. Throughout my Christian life, I have been taught that the name 'Abba' means Daddy and that its use in the Bible means we can approach God in a cuddly and intimate manner. In this case, 'Abba' is likened to the call of a child that is experiencing utter dreadfulness. If you are experiencing pain and abandonment, then be encouraged that you, too, can approach God in this manner. You do not need to pretend that everything is alright.

The Cry to God as 'Father' in the New Testament is not a calm acknowledgement of a universal truth about God's abstract fatherhood.

It is the Child's cry out of a nightmare.

It is the cry of outrage, fear, shrinking away, when faced with the horror of the 'world', yet not simply or exclusively protest, but trust as well.

'Abba Father'

all things are possible to thee....

Former Archbishop of Canterbury Rowan Williams

THE WORLD YOU CREATED IS MEANINGLESS

Another biblical writer that expresses his disappointment with the world is the writer of Ecclesiastes. He is most likely to be King Solomon, the son of King David (mentioned above). We can read his scathing assessment of God's world in Ecclesiastes 1:2-11, and it certainly seems obvious to me that he is going through some sort of dark depression as he writes this. We should not be afraid of uttering our most dismal thoughts to God; he is not offended when we express honesty.

> Smoke, nothing but smoke.
> There's nothing to anything—it's all smoke.
> What's there to show for a lifetime of work,
> a lifetime of working your fingers to the bone?
> One generation goes its way, the next one arrives,
> but nothing changes—it's business as usual for old
> planet earth.
> The sun comes up and the sun goes down,
> then does it again, and again—the same old round.
> The wind blows south, the wind blows north.
> Around and around and around it blows,
> blowing this way, then that—the whirling, erratic wind.
> All the rivers flow into the sea,
> but the sea never fills up.
> The rivers keep flowing to the same old place,
> and then start all over and do it again.
> Everything's boring, utterly boring—
> no one can find any meaning in it.
> Boring to the eye,
> boring to the ear.
> What was will be again,
> what happened will happen again.
> There's nothing new on this earth.
> Year after year it's the same old thing.
> Does someone call out, "Hey, this is new"?
> Don't get excited—it's the same old story.
> Nobody remembers what happened yesterday.
> And the things that will happen tomorrow?
> Nobody'll remember them either.
> Don't count on being remembered.

Ecclesiastes 1:2-11

GOD REPLIES

In the examples above, we have no record of how God responded to the accusation that He has been absent and uncaring. However, in the book of Job, we do find a reply. Job had gone through near-hell; he had lost all of his health and wealth, his family had died, and he was in physical pain. For a while, Job continues to trust in God before finally losing it. Firstly, Job protests his innocence, and then he accuses God of neglecting him and sending him to his death (Job 30:20-23). God's response is awe-inspiring:

And now, finally, God answered Job from the eye of a violent storm. He said:
"Why do you confuse the issue?
Why do you talk without knowing what you're talking about?
Pull yourself together, Job!
Up on your feet! Stand tall!
I have some questions for you,
and I want some straight answers.
Where were you when I created the earth?
Tell me, since you know so much!
Who decided on its size? Certainly you'll know that!
Who came up with the blueprints and measurements?
How was its foundation poured,
and who set the cornerstone,
While the morning stars sang in chorus
and all the angels shouted praise?
And who took charge of the ocean
when it gushed forth like a baby from the womb?
That was me! I wrapped it in soft clouds,
and tucked it in safely at night.

Job 38:1-11

God continues to remind Job of His incredible creation for another two chapters and finishes with:

"Now what do you have to say for yourself?"

Job 40:2

Perhaps we, too, have no idea what we are talking about when we accuse God of neglect. His fantastic handiwork is all around us, and we know so little.

LEARNING FROM OTHER CHRISTIANS

In a recent survey, we asked readers of my blog www.dislocatedchristians.org "When you feel distant from God, what helps you to reconnect with Him?" Here's how our readers responded:

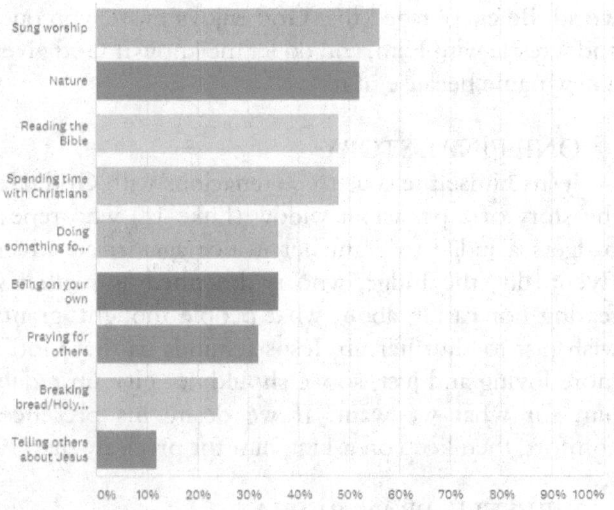

When you feel distant from God, what helps you to reconnect with Him?

Several followers also took the time to leave comments. They suggested: "Waiting reading His word", "Contemplation and working in partnership with other

Christians. Lent groups and bible study groups", "Thankfulness", and one person offered wise advice "All of these sometimes. Sometimes they have the opposite effect."

A NATION OF WRESTLERS
Did you know that the name 'Israel' means 'God-wrestler'? In the book of Genesis, there's a somewhat bizarre story about a man called Jacob (Genesis 32). Jacob spends all night wrestling with an unknown man and refuses to let go until this man gives Jacob his blessing. In the end, Jacob recognises his opponent as God, and God changes Jacob's name to Israel because God is impressed with Jacob/Israel for not giving up. Many years later, Jacob/Israel goes on to father the people of Israel, who become God's chosen nation, called upon to bless the world. Be encouraged that God enjoys those who question and wrestle with Him, and do let me know if God gives you a new name because of it!

ONE FINAL STORY
Jesus himself tells us to be tenacious with God. He told the story of a persistent widow (Luke 18) who repeatedly badgers a judge to grant her justice against an adversary. Eventually, the Judge, who is described as neither God-fearing nor caring about what people thought, grants her wish just to shut her up. Jesus reminds us that God is far more loving and just, so we should not give up requesting him for what we want. If we desire his presence and comfort, then keep on asking him for precisely that.

WRESTLE, PRAY, REPEAT
Father God, we pray that you would reveal yourself to us and become lovingly present in our everyday lives. The world is frightening without you. We want you to be close to us. Draw near, we pray. Amen

5 OLD NEWS

As Christians, we have brilliant news to share. Every person, from each culture and country, can have hope and freedom. Their sins are forgiven, and everything that causes pain and destruction has been overcome. It is incredible, but Jesus' victory over sin and darkness took place a long time ago. Rather than generating excitement, telling people about his death and resurrection can seem like passing on old news.

FAIRY TALES?
Many people think they have heard the gospel story and assume they know all they need to about it. To them, Bible stories can be like fairy tales and are treated more like myths from ancient worlds than life-changing truths. It is assumed that only simple people need to believe them.

Yet, Jesus' death and resurrection are still supremely relevant. Belief in him and the loving relationship that forms once someone gets to know Him personally is to encounter truth, love, and power. He breathes life into every situation.

HOW DO WE MAKE OLD NEWS RELEVANT AGAIN?

In chapter 4 of the book of John, found in the Bible, we see an example of Jesus sharing old news and bringing it to exhilarating life. He encounters a woman who knows part of the story. She's from a minority group that was traditionally excluded from the traditions and knowledge that the Jews benefited from. She's heard two rumours and speaks to Jesus about them. Firstly, she wonders where worship ought to take place. Does she have to go to Jerusalem, or can she worship God in her home region? Secondly, she states her hope that the promised Messiah will come but doesn't know what to expect.

Jesus tells her that she can worship 'wherever and whenever' and that God actively seeks people who honestly adore Him. Then he declares that He is the very Messiah she has heard stories about. He connects the dots for her, and the old tales suddenly become vivid and life-giving.

HAVE YOU EVER BEEN SO EXCITED ABOUT SOMETHING THAT YOU HAVE FORGOTTEN TO EAT?

After Jesus shares this news, the two of them suddenly become very animated and excited. She rushes off to tell everyone she knows about what she has heard and how it makes sense to her now. Jesus is also buzzing. His friends return to find him in this agitated state and tell him to eat. He tells them he can't sit down to eat now; he's sharing old news!

When we share the gospel, though it may seem like old news to some, we get to be like Jesus. We can join the dots for those with questions and partial knowledge of the ways of God. We can tell people that the good news reaches them today and hope and a new life are awaiting them.

Just remember to eat!

6 CRUCIFIED SAVIOUR

Well, this is it, the crux of Christianity. If Jesus weren't a crucified saviour, there would be nothing to believe in except some wise teachings. But He is that greatest of oxymorons, a hero that died and came back to glorious life. He is still the great 'I am'. His death at the hands of the Roman authorities was not the end.

YOU COULDN'T MAKE IT UP

No other religion has a central figure that gives up everything, even their own life, for the sake of others. Even Jesus' return to life is different. He doesn't come back with armies ready to conquer the world but instead appears to regular folk. He leaves them to tell the world about his victory over death before returning to His Father. In the course of history, it would be easy to overlook what He achieved, yet His story is still told; there is never-ending power in His actions.

There are many theories and definitions to explain what Jesus achieved by being crucified. He was sacrificed for us, performed substitutionary atonement and was the Lamb of God. Yet, no matter what you call it or the theological ins and outs, His was a long and torturous death. He suffered. We are saved because he bore the penalty of sin. A practical solution that was painful, necessary, and real.

A DIFFERENT KIND OF HERO
Jesus' death and resurrection do not only seem shocking to us but were a surprise to those who knew Him at the time. They were expecting a different kind of hero too.

A TERRORIST?
One of Jesus' followers, Simon, was a zealot. They were the domestic terrorists of the day, ready and willing to use the sword to overthrow the Roman occupation and end the oppressive taxation of the Jewish people. He may have been anticipating that Jesus would become a military leader and evict the Romans forcibly.

A KING?
Simon was not alone in expecting more action. On the first Palm Sunday, Jesus rode a donkey into Jerusalem while the crowds shouted His praise. They identified him as the Son of David, their revered warrior King from centuries earlier. Were they also hoping that Jesus would oust Herod and reclaim the throne?

A LAW-ABIDING CITIZEN?
The Pharisees were similarly looking forward to the arrival of the Messiah, but they did not recognise that Jesus was the promised one. Instead, they expected a rule follower who would enforce their unnecessary and burdensome purity laws. Jesus was no follower of earthly rules; rather, He came to fulfil the law as the crucified saviour.

A GENIE?
In John 4, there is an interesting (and hard to interpret encounter) between Jesus and a government official. The official approaches Jesus because his son is dying and asks

for him to be healed. Jesus rebukes him in verse 48, saying, 'Unless you people are dazzled by a miracle, you refuse to believe'. It seems the government official was treating Jesus like a genie in a bottle – desiring to be blessed, yet not believing who Jesus really was. This cuts closest to home; do I, too, think of Jesus as someone who does things for me, rather than simply loving, adoring, and believing in Him?

A SURPRISE?

There is one character in the Bible who seems to know Jesus better than any other of the others, and she appears to have much more insight into what He may be up to. This person is Mary, Jesus' Mother. Shortly after the angel Gabriel tells her she is to bear the son of God, she authors the beautiful words of The Magnificat, describing God's promises and what Jesus will do. Here are the words from Luke 1:50 onwards in the New Living Translation:

He shows mercy from generation to generation to all who fear him.

His mighty arm has done tremendous things!

He has scattered the proud and haughty ones.

He has brought down princes from their thrones and exalted the humble.

He has filled the hungry with good things and sent the rich away with empty hands.

He has helped his servant Israel and remembered to be merciful.

For he made this promise to our ancestors, to Abraham and his children forever.

The Magnificat in Luke 1

For all this talk of thrones and generations, Mary also knows that Jesus cares about everyday matters. Later, at the wedding Cana (John 2), she suspects Jesus is capable of more when she informs Him that their hosts have run out of wine. Her advice to the servants is to do whatever He tells them. What gave her this inkling that Jesus could perform miracles? Had he told her plainly, or had her life been so strange up to this point that she was willing to be surprised again.

The biggest shocks came later in her life when she tragically watched Jesus, her son, die a painful death on the cross. What must she have thought? Did she still have hope? Her joy when she saw Him raised from the dead must have been ecstatic. How I would love to talk with Mary about all these things, her life was such a rollercoaster.

WHAT ARE YOU EXPECTING FROM JESUS?

Someone to fight your battles? Do you want Him to join your side and settle political disputes once and for all? Are you seeking a law follower who plays by your rules? Or, are you hoping for a genie to do miracles for you? Can I suggest that you follow Mary's example and prepare yourself to be surprised by Jesus? It is the biggest and best adventure!

Help me, Lord, to seek and know the real Jesus, the Crucified Saviour. Surprise me and lead me on the adventure you have prepared for me.

These words were written by Godfrey Birtill and sum up Jesus' action on the cross beautifully:

When I stop at the cross
I can see the love of God
But I can't see competition
I can't see hierarchy
I can't see pride or prejudice
or the abuse of authority
I can't see lust for power
I can't see manipulation

I can't see rage or anger
or selfish ambition
But I can't see unforgiveness
I can't see hate or envy
I can't see stupid fighting
or bitterness, or jealousy.
I can't see empire building
I can't see self-importance
I can't see backstabbing
Or vanity or arrogance.
I see surrender, sacrifice, salvation,
humility, righteousness, faithfulness, grace, forgiveness
Love Love Love……..
When I Stop!….at the cross
I can see the love of God.

Copyright Godfrey Birtill http://elyrics.net

7 SERVANT KING

There is heaps of theology out there, in books, courses, articles and videos about Christ as the Servant King. Most of the material focuses on chapters 40 to 55 in the book of Isaiah in the Bible. Consequently, when I came to write this post, I wondered what contribution I could make to a topic that has been written about so much already.

The difference is perhaps that I have had servants; well, kind of. Please don't write me off for this; I have spent over three years living in Kathmandu, Nepal and having staff in our house is a means of providing much-needed jobs. In the case of our Cook, we offered her a home too, since she lived with us. We don't call them servants, but some of the ideas are the same.

In my experience, then, a servant gives up some of their life to further yours. Having staff is a highly intimate experience as they get to see you close up, all your good and bad points. They know about the chocolate you've hidden in the fridge, wash your underwear, and observe how you discipline and bring up your children. They take a fair bit of getting used to.

I've felt a strong sense of teamwork with the staff I've had. If I have to host an event at our house, they are a reassuring presence as we work together to run the occasion. Good communication is essential, and I have to trust them; otherwise, I drive them mad by micro-managing everything they do. They are my link to the real, local world, and I am their link to the ex-pat world. We learn from each other and ask a lot of questions.

So what does all this mean for our understanding of Jesus as the Servant King? I believe he, too, wishes to enter our household and participate in our intimate family lives. We see this longing in Revelation 3:20, in a letter written to Christians: 'Here I am! I stand at the door and knock. If anyone hears my voice and opens the door, I will come in'. He wants to be in the midst of everything going on with us, the good and messy. I suppose he could send angels instead, but he opts to join us Himself.

But Jesus is not only a servant; He is King too. Therefore he has standards and responsibilities he cannot violate. When He serves us, He won't submit to our will over His own. He only helps us in those areas of our life that also further his Kingdom. I can instruct my staff to do things that are not good for me, such as serving me alcohol at all times of the day, but Jesus is not that type of Servant. He only does what is good for us.

Just like the way in which my staff connect me to the local world, Jesus connects us to His Kingdom, which consists of spiritual forces we can't see clearly on our own. We can learn from him and invite Him to influence our daily lives so that He becomes a reassuring presence we trust and rely on.

We have the incredible opportunity to invite Jesus into

our lives and to allow him to see everything that goes on. Why not permit him to further those areas of your life that build His Kingdom? And, no matter what, keep on communicating with Him; everything He does is for our good.

8 LIVING SACRIFICE

'The living sacrifice', that's Christ. Why is it necessary that Christ is both living and a sacrifice?

'A living sacrifice', that's us. Why do we need to become living sacrifices?

THE ~~LIVING~~ SACRIFICE

We have done many things wrong, but Jesus paid the price for them by dying in our place; He's the sacrifice. But if he hadn't come back to life afterwards, there would be no victory over the darkness and sins that plague us. Christ overcame, and we get to share in his triumph. We are no longer slaves to sin (Romans 6:6). Wonderfully, since he is now alive, we can talk to him, and he prays for us (Isaiah 53:12).

THE LIVING ~~SACRIFICE~~

Christ came to earth and lived a perfect life; he was a fully living human being. Consequently, he can identify with all our hardships and temptations. He knows what it is like to be ridiculed, ostracised and despised. But if he were only a living example for us, we would still need to pay the penalty for our sins, which is death. Jesus told his followers he was the lamb of God, meaning that he was the required sacrifice. He would be either mad or evil if he hadn't followed up on these words and died in our place. Thankfully, he became our sacrifice.

WHAT ABOUT US? WE ARE INVITED TO BECOME LIVING SACRIFICES; WHY WOULD WE DO THIS?

A ~~LIVING~~ SACRIFICE

This would be our state without Christ. We are so impure and God so holy and righteous that we cannot approach him independently. Instead, we would remain in darkness and decay. Even if they looked like 'sacrifices', our efforts or works would not be enough to save us.

A LIVING ~~SACRIFICE~~

To carry on living without regard or appreciation for what Christ has done for us or oblivious to the freedom He has won for us is desperately sad. Living selfishly, to please only ourselves, leads to ostracism from God. Instead, we can offer our lives to God in grateful love and appreciation for all He has done for us. God does not coerce us; we give ourselves to Him because we choose to. This is our sacrifice.

OUR CALLING IS TO BECOME LIVING SACRIFICES TO GOD

Romans 12 describes how this looks. When we give ourselves to God and turn away from anything impure, he has so much to offer us in return. Our minds will be transformed so that we'll know more and more of how good and pleasing His ways are. This isn't mind-control but a renewal of healthy thoughts that line up with how the creator of the world sees things. We'll find new meaning in Christ's family and discover God's particular purposes for us. It is exciting. God has a plan for you. Don't hold back; offer yourself to Him. He is such a safe pair of hands, and together we'll see evil overcome.

We can leap for joy because of that.

9 UNCHANGING CREATOR

God's always doing something new; it's his habit. He made seven hundred and six thousand eyeballs today, each of them unique, and those are just the human ones.

This attribute of God floors me. Every new idea is His. Every ingenious solution to a problem is inspired by Him. Made in His image, each time we find a way to solve a problem and feel that rush of satisfaction, we are like Him.

He sustains all things by His word. That's the safe, secure, unchanging part. The laws of nature, for instance, but He can always do something new with them. We're discovering more of them each day. Our next stop is Mars.

Within His rules for life, there is countless variation. Over sixty thousand species of tree; just imagine each of their leaves. Every one unique yet identifiable.

Our unchanging-creator-God is the greatest hope for the future. As we in our sinful state keep on creating more problems, God, in his abundant originality, finds ways to save us. And best of all, we can join him as he does this. He chooses to share His creativity with us and works through His church and us.

No matter the concern, climate change, fake news, pandemics and conflict. Have faith; there are magnificent solutions to each, but He asks us to seek Him and hold on to His unchanging attributes to discover them: love, faith and truth.

10 DIVINE HUMAN

It's easy to think that Jesus was some sort of hybrid. A one-of-a-kind blend of divinity and humanity, like mixing blue and yellow to make green. As if he were an utterly different colour to us.

But no, he was fully human and fully divine—Blue and yellow.

God in human form is not unique to Christianity. Other religions celebrate gods who take on mortality; they make God in our image, rather than the other way round. I live in Nepal, so I'm familiar with Hindu gods. Greek and Roman myths contain many more examples too.

Yet, in these stories, the gods become human to maximise their physicality. They put on a body so they can wage war against humans. Or, they want to indulge in human sensuality, and a human body permits them to sleep with whomever they desire.

JESUS WAS UTTERLY DIFFERENT.

He took on a human form to empathise with our weaknesses and know what it is like to be tempted. He learnt obedience and made himself completely vulnerable as a baby. To begin with, He couldn't feed himself, talk or control any aspect of His life. Furthermore, He didn't choose to be born to a wealthy family but arrived in obscurity.

A HELPLESS GOD IS UNIQUE.
You couldn't make it up. Only God could have come up with such a strategy to be with us. What an incredible friend we have in Jesus.

For we do not have a high priest who is unable to empathise with our weaknesses, but we have one who has been tempted in every way, just as we are—yet he did not sin. Let us then approach God's throne of grace with confidence, so that we may receive mercy and find grace to help us in our time of need. Hebrews 4:15- 16

He learned obedience from what he suffered. Hebrews 5:8

One of the most powerful and memorable meditations I have done was a sensory imagining of what Jesus went through in the wilderness following his baptism.

At once, the Spirit sent him out into the wilderness, and he was in the wilderness forty days, being tempted by Satan. He was with the wild animals, and angels attended him. Mark 1:12 – 13

It was cold at night; Jesus would have had goosebumps.

He would have sweated during the day; soon, he would have been able to smell Himself.

The sun's glare across the bare earth would have hurt His eyes.

He would have missed the voices of His family, and at night, He might have felt scared by the sound of desert animals.

Of course, He would have felt ravenous too.

He endured so much more, and I encourage you to meditate on everything He went through. All of his sufferings were voluntary.

Jesus was a divine human; it will take me more than a lifetime to get my head around it.

11 JEALOUS GOD

Imagine you're an artist, and you've spent the last few years completing your masterpiece. You're delighted with it, it is your best work, and as you gaze at it, you know the countless hours you spent on it were worth it.

Your friend, a gallery curator, visits, and you show them the painting. They agree it is your finest work and are eager to show it in their gallery.

On the exhibition's opening night, you wander the showrooms looking at the other paintings on display. Your piece has been given pride of place, and it is the best artwork in the gallery.

As the visitors pour in, you notice them gasp with delight as they look upon your work. No one knows that you are the artist, so you edge a little closer to the party discussing your work to hear what they think.

"It's incredible!"

"I love it."

"… but surely it can't have been painted by this unknown artist; we'd have seen their work before."

"I think it's one of the master artists playing a prank on us; they're displaying their work under an alias."

"… or perhaps this upstart painter discovered this piece and wants everyone to think it's their own work."

As you stand there listening to them, emotions overwhelm you. Why does no one believe an unknown artist could have produced this painting? You simply want to be recognised for your creative work.

Does a jealous God feel like this?

Consider now that you're a musician and you're in love. You write a song for your boyfriend and invite him to your house, where you have a grand piano, to play it for him.

As you sing it to him, you see that he loves it. His eyes fill with tears, and he is enraptured. Your boyfriend asks you to play it over and over before pulling out his phone and asking if he may record it.

"Of course", you agree.

Once he's captured the song on his device, he thanks you profusely and tells you that he will listen to the music every day. He anticipates a lifetime of pleasure listening to it.

He leaves shortly after, and as the front door clicks shut, you can't help feeling that the evening didn't go as planned. You wanted him to love you, not the song.

Does a jealous God feel like this too?

12 FOOLISH WISDOM

You don't have to go far on the internet, to find plentiful examples of posts in which Christians are accused of being idiots. Sometimes these attacks come in the form of lengthy arguments; in others, the accusations are short attacks full of swear words and vitriol. Why is it that so many Christians cherish the wisdom they find in the Bible, but that same knowledge seems like complete nonsense to those outside the faith? Why the mismatch?

IT'S JUST LIKE LIVING IN CORINTH
The situation we Christians find ourselves in is described well in the Bible. In the book of Corinthians, Paul, a teacher and preacher, explains to the believers who live in Corinth that God purposely chose to turn things upside down. It was God's desire that ideas and actions that seem foolish to many might hold the secret to deep eternal wisdom.

To preach the message of the cross seems like sheer nonsense to those who are on their way to destruction, but to us who are being saved, it is the mighty power of God released within us. For it is written:
I will dismantle the wisdom of the wise and I will

invalidate the intelligence of the scholars.

So, where is the wise philosopher who understands? Where is the expert scholar who comprehends? And where is the skilled debater of our time who could win a debate with God? Hasn't God demonstrated that the wisdom of this world system is utter foolishness?

1 Corinthians 1:18-20 (The Passion)

Corinth was home to many famous philosophers and debaters, admired for the flamboyant expositions they delivered in public. These debaters won fans by presenting amusing critiques of commonly held beliefs; however, their ideas often had no substance in practice. Similarly, we might enjoy listening to a political comedian today who can humorously point out what is wrong with things as they are but may not offer a feasible solution. Their worldly arguments, Paul suggests, are no match for God's wisdom, which is the key to life. Though we may speak the gospel quietly and humbly, often through our actions rather than flashy discourse, Paul assures us it is more valuable than any wisdom of the world.

EVERYTHING IS UPSIDE DOWN

So what was God thinking when he decided to overturn the world's ideas of philosophy and knowledge? He's made life hard for Christians because we have been ridiculed and, at times, persecuted for the presumed folly of our ways. These verses in Corinthians, which come immediately after the passage above, offer some answers.

For in his wisdom, God designed that all the world's wisdom would be insufficient to lead people to the discovery of himself. He took great delight in baffling the wisdom of the world by using the simplicity of preaching the story of the cross to save those who believe it. For the Jews constantly demand to see miraculous signs, while those who are not Jews constantly cling to the world's wisdom, but we preach the crucified Messiah. The Jews stumble over him and the rest of the world sees him as foolishness. But for those who have been chosen to follow him, both Jews and Greeks, he is God's mighty power, God's true wisdom, and our Messiah. For the "foolish" things of God have proven to be wiser than human wisdom. And the "feeble" things of God have proven to be far more powerful than any human ability.

1 Corinthians 1:21-31 (The Passion)

Paul makes special mention of Jews who found the whole idea of a Crucified Saviour having the power to save anyone ridiculous. There are many people through the ages who would agree with their assessment. It could be said that any of the names for God I've chosen to examine in this book about The Oxymoronic God seem irrational (Jealous God, Divine Human, Unchanging Creator, Living Sacrifice, Servant King, Absent Father, Merciful Judge, Lion & Lamb, Prince of Peace), yet, I believe these word combinations strike against each other in the manner of flints. For a moment, a spark appears that allows us to see God more clearly.

God did not want anyone excluded from hearing the good news, so he made it plain and simple; this is not the way of the world. The simple wisdom of God that Christ died and rose again is not complicated. If it were more complex so that only those with advanced degrees could understand it, they might be tempted to sell their knowledge. Even today, there are cults and conferences with hefty signup fees promising the secret to an abundant life.

God's wisdom is offered to us as a gift. We can't earn it, so no one can boast that they are more deserving than anyone else. We simply need to accept the gift. Again, this is not the usual way of doing things.

STILL THINK WE'RE CRAZY?

If you remain unconvinced and think Christians are deluded, then I encourage you to get to know Jesus. To be fair, he was pretty unconventional and turned the lives of those he encountered upside down, but He is all the more incredible for it. He wasn't a nutcase who damaged his followers by lying to them; instead, their lives flourished as they encountered His love. I suggest you begin by reading the gospels: the books of Matthew, Mark, Luke and John in the Bible. There are many translations of the Bible, so it's best to get hold of an up to date translation; The Message or The Passion are both excellent.

THERE'S HOPE

You are not alone if you already believe in Christ and His foolish wisdom. I can't stop the online vitriol you may encounter, but it will end one day, and everything will make perfect sense.

13 SHEPHERD LORD

If it were up to me, I would give myself a discount on concert tickets. I am so short and always find myself standing behind someone tall. I don't get the same experience at concerts that others do. I wouldn't say that I feel scared in a crowd, but there's definitely a feeling of claustrophobia, and I know of other people my height who avoid crowds altogether.

WHAT IS IT LIKE TO BE A SHEEP?
Sheep are short too, and their view is often obstructed. Without a shepherd, it's easy for them to find themselves lost and in dangerous situations. Thankfully, shepherds are much taller than sheep; they can anticipate trouble and keep them out of harm's way.

WHAT IS JESUS LIKE?
In the Bible, Jesus' followers are likened to sheep, and Jesus promises to be their shepherd. We're to follow him, and Jesus promises that we'll recognise his voice.

Not only is Jesus our shepherd, which traditionally has been a lowly profession, but he's Lord too. It's as if the shepherd is also the landowner. He knows the land we graze on and is aware of the pitfalls. When we follow him, he knows exactly where the best pastures are and can guide us to them along the best routes. This is what Psalm 23, known familiarly as 'The Lord is my Shepherd', is all about.

A ROD AND A STAFF. WHAT ARE THEY FOR?

Psalm 23 also tells us that our Shepherd Lord holds a rod and a staff. Shepherds used rods to beat off animals that may attack the sheep and hooked a staff around a sheep's neck to pull it out of trouble. Using both a rod and staff means the shepherd protects the sheep from external threats and their own internal waywardness. I love this. Jesus, our shepherd, fends off our attackers and helps us out of tight-spots of our own making. How reassuring!

WHAT DOES THIS MEAN FOR US?

We're safe then. When troubles seem to surround us, and we can't see a way through them, we can look to Jesus, who has a much greater perspective. He'll guide us to places where he'll know we'll flourish and thrive, and if danger comes, he can rescue us from every situation. Perhaps he'll even lift us on his shoulders so we can enjoy his perspective. I want to stick close to him, our shepherd Lord.

14 SILENT CHRISTIANS

I've written this book because I love God and want my readers to see Him in fresh ways. I'm constantly surprised by how God continues to defy my expectations and breaks out of any box I might put Him in. I want to share these thoughts with my readers; I appreciate you reading these chapters. However, this chapter is for me. I'm trying to work out if I should be silent or not. If I should write about a particular topic or whether it's not for me. Of course, I'm sharing my thinking here as I hope you'll benefit too, and perhaps you'll share some of your wisdom with me.

This chapter is part of a book looking at oxymorons. Oxymorons are pairs of words that seem to contradict each other, i.e. old news, but are frequently used together as a single term.

SHOULD CHRISTIANS BE SILENT?

Speaking up on issues is something that Christians seem to stumble over. Sometimes we're too quiet on topics, such as the war in Yemen, and other times we are too loud. We bombard society with our beliefs while failing to listen to the hurting world around us—gay marriage and abortion spring to mind.

How can we get the balance right? I want the world to know we Christians care, but I don't want to be part of a collective voice that goes on and on so that eventually, society longs for us to shut up.

WHAT ADVICE DOES THE BIBLE GIVE US?
Well, it's wise to know when to be silent. Only fools go on and on (Prov 10:19-22, 11:13 and 12:33). Being quiet benefits us and those around us (Prov 13:3 and James 3). Generally, when instruction is given to God-followers collectively, we are advised to be humble and let our actions do the talking (Micah 6:8 and 1 Thes 4:11-12).

BUT SHOULDN'T WE SPEAK UP FOR THOSE WHO HAVE NO VOICE?
Yes, but generally, God gives these types of instructions to specific people at specific times. The famous verse from Proverbs 31 quoted above (that has meant a lot to me as I know it has to many) was spoken by a mother to her son. Her son was a ruler and King.

Can we generalise those words to apply to all Christians all the time? Probably not if we use them as an excuse for internet rants. Yet, we're told all scripture is God-breathed and useful for teaching (2 Tim 3:16). If the Holy Spirit at a specific time and for a particular reason quickens our heart by bringing that verse to us, we should humbly and prayerfully accept it as a calling to raise our voice. My quandary is whether God is calling me to apply that verse now.

SO WHAT SHOULD CHRISTIANS TALK ABOUT?
We should stick to what we know (Acts 4:20), and if you know God, that qualifies you to proclaim the good news of the gospel (1 Cor 11:26 and 1 John 1:3).

AND FINALLY.
Speak in love; otherwise, you'll become an irritation, and your words will lose all meaning (1 Cor 13:1). I am confident we can do this with God's help and the Holy Spirit. Please pray for me as I seek God's leading; thank you.

ABOUT THE AUTHOR

ABOUT THE AUTHOR

Anna is an Army wife and mother of a son and a daughter. Following a two-year posting to Nepal with her husband, who serves with the Gurkhas (soldiers from Nepal), she founded and runs the Christian charity Women Without Roofs - Nepal. She blogs at www.dislocatedchristians.org and has also written the following books:

Come with me to Kathmandu: 12 powerful stories of women's courageous faith in Nepal (due to be published to mark International Women's Day in March 2023)

Destination Transformation: A forty-day journey to change the world, written for people with baggage

Destination Transformation: Study Guide for Small Groups: A six-session study guide for small groups of people with baggage who want to change the world

The British Gurkhas After Resettlement: How they can successfully contribute towards Nepal's development from the UK